TIME OUT!

What's the Plan?

Ron Kunkel

ISBN 978-1-63814-078-8 (Paperback)
ISBN 978-1-63814-079-5 (Digital)

Covenant Books, Inc.
11661 Hwy 707
Murrells Inlet, SC 29576
www.covenantbooks.com

W hat's the plan for us? What's the plan for me? How one day changed my thoughts on what my reason is here on earth. March 21, 2020, is a day that will forever go down as the scariest, most painful, most remembered, and maybe one of the most important days of my life.

The *time-out* in the title is relevant as my clock needed to stop. Whether I wanted it to stop or not, it needed to stop. The time stopped with one second left on the clock, waiting to find out if this was game over for me, or if more time would be put back on the clock for me. As you will see, I wasn't in any position to make that determination and our clock manager from above was the one to determine how long my game will continue to go. As a youth coach of many teams in my hometown, sports metaphors are the easiest ways, at times, to get my message across to others.

What's the plan? Man, that question came up time and time again through my couple day story. "God must still have plans for you." "Sounds like you have unfinished business here in this life." "The big guy upstairs must have favor on you." "What are you going to do with the extra opportunity God gave you?" These are all things that I was told before even leaving the hospital after my whole ordeal that started on March 21.

I invite you to take a walk with me through an event that will change my life forever and the days after that would shape what it is that I'm supposed to do with the rest of my life. I don't have the answers. I don't even know what the questions are, honestly. I'm looking for a sign. I thought about waiting for that sign, but also realized that he hasn't given me a sign to not write this book, which at this time is the only thing I can think about doing with what I've gone through. A very close friend of mine texted me a couple of days after March 21 and said, "…could save some lives to just share it as I am always nervous of something like that happening to me…maybe that is also God's plan for the experience."

So, I look forward to walking with you through my long couple of days and then reviewing possibilities of what "The Plan" is.

*****

Before we get into what happened on March 21, I thought it would be very important to explain some other things that happened over the past two years that became a part of my most recent opportunity to appreciate the grace of God.

Christmas Eve of 2017, I woke up in the middle of the night with extreme neck and upper back pain. I literally thought I was dying. The pain was horrible and would last about twenty minutes, hot and heavy, and then it would subside. After this happened, I didn't know what the heck was going on. With an attempt of going back to bed, many things were racing through my head. Was it just a kink in the neck or a slight pinched nerve? Was I having something worse like a heart attack? I didn't know. I only knew that I had never had that pain before and have never been in so much pain for a stretch of twenty minutes in my entire life. I looked up on my phone the symptoms of a heart attack and it really did not fit what I was going through.

Well, two hours later, I was up going through another twenty minutes of ungodly pain. What I noticed was that it was almost twenty minutes to the second, both times. After twenty minutes, the pain would just go away, and I was able to breathe and relax again as if nothing happened. The pain would be a shooting pain up my neck and into the lower part of the back of my head. It would continue halfway down my back and into my shoulders. That is where the pain would stop, but there would be tingling on both arms all the way down to the fingers.

I had one more episode prior to everyone waking up Christmas morning. When Christmas morning came, things seemed to have subsided, as I really didn't have any issues all morning. Shortly after eating a large Christmas meal with my family and my in-laws, while I was cleaning the turkey carcass, I could feel the same sensation coming on. It always seemed to give me a one to two-minute notice prior to its arrival. I slowly got up and made my way to the bedroom to lay on the bed, to try to prepare for it and try to relax. That didn't work. It hit as hard as it did each time during the night. The only thing I could think of doing was to try to take a hot shower. Though this eased some of the direct pain, the length of time was still almost the same. With barely enough hot water left from the shower, I was able to stop, get out, and make my way to the bed for the last portion of the pain that was more bearable.

Unfortunately, it takes a while to fill the water heater with more hot water, and when I needed to return to the shower with another incident in about an hour's time, there wasn't enough hot water to be very effective or to help ease the pain in any way. It's Christmas Day. I'm going through all this pain on a day that our family just stays home and stays together. At this time, I did nothing but try to relax. The pain was the same each time. The pain always lasted about the same amount of time. The tingling was present each time as well, and this becomes the relevant part to March 21, 2020.

I went through another night of being up almost every two hours with this for twenty minutes at a time. I finally just moved out to the couch, so I would stop waking up my wife, Jen. The next day, I went into the walk-in to see if they could figure out what was wrong. They didn't see anything but were able to give me a little something for the pain. I'm never much for taking anything for pain but thought I would give these a try and they did help a little bit.

I ended up missing about a week of work because of the constant on and off pain that I was still going through. The pain was less, but the frequency stayed about the same. As a youth basketball coach during winter, I couldn't hardly sit on the bench during a game without dying of pain. In practice, I was forced, most nights, of sitting on a chair on the side of the court, blurting out instructions instead of showing by example. This was getting old.

Come early February, I was able to get an appointment with a spine and neuroscience specialist. I was not thrilled about this other than an opportunity to ease the pain. Nobody touches my neck, as that is a phobia of mine. I was worried about what this visit was going to be about. It ended up being a lot of questions and ultimately an agreement to do an open MRI in the upcoming weeks. I was good with this and will skip a claustrophobics' experience of how that MRI went. We did though, determine afterwards that the pain appeared to be coming from a three-inch bruise on the spinal cord near the C2, C3, and C4 vertebrae. I was told a bruised spinal cord doesn't heal and was put on temporary pain medicine and had to make changes in my life to make sure I took things easy and tried not to stress that area of the neck. Things eventually got better, and I learned to live with the occasional pain, discomfort and tingling sensations.

Prior to this neck thing happening, I had gotten back on a regular rotation of seeing my personal doctor. This put things to a halt of going to the doctor, because less than six months later, I was rushed to the emergency room by a friend to get my gallbladder quickly removed before it burst. The neck pain months ago didn't seem like that big of a deal anymore, after going through the pain of what a near-bursting gallbladder presents. While the gallbladder removal really doesn't have any effect on the rest of the story, it was my first major surgery and hospital stay that I've ever had. This did help me appreciate what medical workers go through and understand the miracles that happen day in and day out, by them figuring out what is wrong and determining what it takes to make things better. Less than twelve hours after surgery, I was sitting at my baseball team's tournament game in a nearby town, cheering them on quietly from afar to make sure I kept my excitement levels down. The next day, the boys won the championship game and I was fortunate enough to be sitting in my car, behind the outfield fence, to watch my youngest son make a game winning on the run catch in center field to end the game. To see all his teammates and friends run out to center field and jumping up and down was a moment in my mind that I will never forget.

So, with the extra gallbladder surgery that was not part of the plan, the follow-up appointments that went with that, and a revisit to the spine and neurologist specialist, it seemed like I was doing plenty of doctoring for the last two years. Unfortunately looking back now, none of them were for a well-visit appointment or for preventative measures. I probably went way too long since my last regular appointment, so now this is where the story of March 21 is ready to start.

*****

As of writing this, I am a forty-five-year-old man that cannot sit down or take a time-out. My wife, Jen, and I have been together for twenty years and married for seventeen of those. Though she's always been a strong person, has been extremely supportive of my choices in life and very helpful with my medical issues to date, I was always fearful that she would think that I'm weak with my recent medical issues. I don't think anyone that I know really understood the pain that I went through with my spinal cord issues. She never said a word or suggested anything, but as a husband that wants to be strong for his wife and family, my record was continuing to come into question, regarding physical strength, from my regards anyways.

Jen and I have a sixteen-year-old daughter named Jaicee. She's a junior in high school, driving her own car, and working at a local pizza market for some friends of ours. She is a great student, strong in faith, and plays volleyball on the school team in fall. Even though she spends most of her evenings in her room, doing homework or listening to music, I still feel that she and I have that special relationship that a father and daughter typically have. I miss seeing her more, but also love the fact that she is making her own decisions and being her own person. She's been extremely fortunate to already have taken two mission trips to El Salvador and she looks forward to her next one.

We also have a fourteen-year-old son named Jorey. He's an eighth-grader this year and participated in Bronco baseball, junior high football and basketball on the school teams this year. He's maybe the smartest kid that I know, almost to the point of being annoying. He beats us at any mind games, can solve a Rubik's Cube in less than forty-five seconds and remembers everything. He's one of the shortest kids in his class, but that doesn't stop him from putting his shoulder pads out there in a football game or occasionally getting stuck guarding a kid, twelve inches taller than him, on the basketball court. We've learned recently that he expects perfection from himself, apparently as Jen would say, isn't too far from his father.

Our youngest child is a ten-year-old son named Quillan. He goes by Q by everyone but his mother. He is all sports all the time. Though my oldest son is a good athlete, Q centers his entire life around sports. This past year he played flag football, baseball, and basketball with his friends for school. He plays on two different traveling baseball teams, one with his class and one with the class in front of him. He's extremely quick and one of the smartest players that I've ever seen at this age, understanding things as they are happening and reacting accordingly at that time. He's also very good at getting his entire team involved, and in basketball has learned that passing is better than shooting already. Anybody can shoot a ball, but those that are willing to pass up a decent shot to give someone a better shot at the age of ten, I think are pretty special.

We have two house cats. The first one, I got suckered into and the other one, I think I got, tricked into. Opening the front door and leaving it open does honestly come to mind at times. Good cats, just not a cat-hair guy.

A little bit about me: I grew up like all three of my kids. I loved being alone like my daughter. I grew up in a churchgoing family where I was eventually able to start making my own religious decisions when I was a junior in high school. Like my oldest son, I've been a perfectionist when it comes to presentations or when meeting the expectations of myself and others. Failures happened often, but to me, it was used as a motivation to only get better at anything. Even at a young age, losing was fine, but not something I wanted to form a habit of. Plateauing has never been an acceptable term or practice in my life, whether that is for me, my children, or for the kids that I coach. Like my youngest son, my world revolved around sports or a ball, like most of his time.

I coach a lot of stuff. Football is my least favorite to coach, so I only was a flag football coach for four years and starting last year, I no longer coach any football.

Baseball is what everyone assumes is my favorite thing to coach or be around. They are wrong, but I am most heavily involved with our town program regarding baseball. I currently run our boys' city league baseball program, which provides ball for any boy between first grade and sixth grade. I'm responsible for every aspect of this league. I've been trying to find a replacement for the last three years, but regardless of what happens, moving forward, I do believe this needs to be my last season. When I took over doing this, seven years ago, we also started a travel team group for kids that wanted to play more and on weekends. I have coached our 14U travel team for the last seven years. I have coached our 12U travel team for the last six years. I help with my youngest son's 11U team as I can, as well. I'm in my second year of being the school Bronco coach and was just asked to be a varsity assistant coach this season. Besides the three travel teams I mentioned above, our town also has three younger travel teams. I am the president, secretary, and treasurer of all travel teams to make sure everyone gets into tournaments, tournaments are paid for and all groups are a cohesive unit. Some may say that I'm a control freak. Maybe. What I am though is someone that wants things to run smoothly. Helping with all teams allows someone to make sure all of them are running smoothly with limited politics involved. Baseball is a lot right now, and that will be changing soon, as well. I need to give some things up and prioritize the stuff I don't completely give up.

Lastly, I coach basketball. This has always been my greatest sports passion. Whether as a kid, as a young adult, or now coaching through these kids I have. I have no greater passion outside my family, than coaching kids in basketball. I have coached my oldest son's team for the last four years and not to take anything away from any other kid, this has been the most enjoyable coaching job I've ever had. As these kids are heading into high school, they have become my friends. I'll never forget the pictures I got to take with each of them individually after the last tournament that I'll ever coach them in. As a small school in the area, we went from a team of "What the heck is going on?" to a team that "holds our own and can beat the big schools" in the area. They work hard, and if that's the best quality that I gave them, then I'm satisfied with that. We discuss often, things that may be relevant to basketball but are also important parts of life outside basketball.

I also coach my youngest son's fifth-grade school team and help with his travel team. Man, this kid can pass and shoot. I was a good player growing up, but he's better than I ever was at this age. Even now, I struggle to still beat him in a game of one-on-one, but the streak is still alive. I don't believe in letting someone win. My boys need to earn a win if they are going to beat me.

I remember growing up, waiting for my dad to come up from the barn. I would be done with my chores and then try to start shooting buckets in the driveway before he would come walking through. He worked a full-time job all day and then came home to a family of six and had milking to do on a small hobby farm. Though I was able to help with fieldwork and take care of things around the house as the oldest son, milking was still something he had to do. Most nights after walking up from the barn, past the basketball hoop to the house, he would just walk right on by or maybe stop for a bit and watch, but too tired to play. It never bothered me because I knew at a young age that my dad worked hard to even give me a chance to own a basketball, a glove, and a football. I knew he was tired.

Some nights he would stop and play a game of pig. He was a good shooter; I maybe wasn't yet while I was in fifth and sixth grade. I honestly don't remember ever beating him, but it didn't matter. I was probably as tall or taller than him by sixth grade and one night when he walked through, he asked if I wanted to play one-on-one. This was not a common request, as I only remember playing a couple of games against him. This was the night I first beat my dad. I had to earn it though and that's why my boys need to earn beating me. Though I wasn't a pure shooter at that time, I spent a ton of time handling the ball and working on unusual shots around the basket. It was close the whole time, but in the end, I finally did it. He never played one-on-one with me again. I always felt like he did it to make me better and once I passed him, it was time for me to start working on something else. Do not just play people you know you can beat.

What he taught me was an ethic of working hard and making sure I was practicing more than anyone else. In all the years of playing youth and high school football, baseball, and basketball, not once did he say anything negative about how I played. If I had a rough game, I would still get the simple "Good job" and he would leave it alone. I needed to work hard on this as a coach and a father. My mindset as a player was to not lose, to not let anyone down, to not make a mistake, and to lead by example to all those coming up behind me. Kids know when they do something wrong. They don't make mistakes in a game on purpose. They know they lost a game. What they don't need is someone telling them they are failure because of one game, one play, one match, one tournament. What they need is encouragement and someone telling them what needs to be worked on if they want to get over that hump next time. Then help them work on what needs to be done.

*****

So, for the last year or so, my neck has been pretty good. I've learned to take it easy and I rarely take one of my pain pills. It has only been some extreme situations that have bothered it up until the last couple weeks. A long hilly walk down to Horseshoe Canyon when we visited the Grand Canyon area last summer was a hard walk. We also visited the Noah's Ark Museum in Kentucky this past Christmas and the walking up and down ramps and just the sheer length of time walking was also hard. Outside those two unusual occasions, it's really been pretty good.

On the evening of Thursday, March 19, the boys asked if I wanted to play a game of two-on-one basketball with them. This is usually something that I've still been able to do and still can beat them. We usually play a game to ten and win by two. By my second shot, I realized that my neck was going to act up on me for this game and it was already pretty painful. It had been a while since it bothered me that much playing basketball. I told the boys that I probably wouldn't be able to play the rest of the game, but they really wanted to play, so I fought through it.

The pain was almost unbearable. It was the same pain that I always used to get. It started each time in the upper neck area, moved up into my head, down my back, across my shoulders, and into my upper chest. I could feel my fingers were a little tingly, so this was nothing out of the ordinary for me, and what I used to go through. It had just been a long time since I had it this bad.

As much as I wanted to quit, I also know that if this thing was coming back, this may be the last time in a while that I would get to play with them. The boys are good enough to take full advantage of someone that can't play much defense and really couldn't dribble. I would just shoot every time they handed me the ball and they would work the ball in low and make nice passes to eat me up with layups. There was really nothing I could do. Like I mentioned before, I don't let my kids win. I don't let anyone win. I may, at times, let them think they can win, but then finish them off as I would try to do with anyone else. I always ask what motivation there is for someone if someone else always just lets them win. I want my kids to improve, not be satisfied that they won when I wasn't trying. It's maybe a flaw, but it is the method I use. The closer they get to beating me, the more they want to beat me. This causes them to practice longer and play harder to get to that point of being able to finally win.

I lost that game by a score of 10–3. Yes, I remember the score and I wasn't really thrilled about it. Only the second time they've beat me, but by far, the worst that I've ever done. Win or lose, we always say, "Good game." After that, I had to go into the house and take one of those hot showers that got me through the pain a couple of years ago. I was quickly able to ease the pain and get my breathing under control, which helps relax my nerves. Now I was just concerned about how bad it was, did I do something to tweak this again and how long was this going to last this time?

*****

In a time where the coronavirus was in full throttle, many people were being quarantined from their jobs, the kids were home from school indefinitely, and everyone was instructed to engage in social distancing by staying home or keeping a distance of six feet or more from anyone not within their household.

Very seldom do we have a weekend where we don't have a sporting event for one of the kids. Basketball season ended abruptly with the virus and baseball season has been put on hold indefinitely. My kids don't go to school right now and are learning from teachers online. My wife has been working at home for the last week and I've been working, but our office is all spread out to keep our six feet separation from others.

I have been bugging my wife and daughter for months to allow me to put up some paneling in our guest bathroom that I got from my previous job. I didn't want it to go to waste and I just wanted to accent one wall in that small bathroom. The actual width of the wall is only about six feet wide. I needed to remove the base trim that was on the wall and I needed to remove the towel bar. I also needed to remove the electrical outlet plate and loosen the outlet from the wall, so I could put the paneling behind it. Overall, I thought this project would take me no longer than two hours to finish with much of that being prep work, tool set up in the garage, and cleanup time when I was done.

I started my project around ten o'clock that morning. Within ten minutes, the bathroom wall was ready for me to start applying the paneling. Each piece is about six inches tall and each piece would just need to be cut a little to fit the width of the wall. I took a little time to set up the saw and tools I needed in the garage. I brought in the compressor and nail gun into the bathroom that is just inside the door, between the house and the garage.

Within minutes, I had four pieces up and was rolling along with no issues. By piece number five, I had to set it down and go into my bathroom at the other end of the house because my neck started to hurt so bad. With the pain coming into the areas of my body that I've already explained, I realized that it was back in my life and that I needed to take a short hot shower to calm it down. I was able to minimize the pain quite quickly.

I got out of the shower and went back to work, as it took me months to convince them that I should finish this wall, I couldn't leave it a third-of-the-way done now.

I was able to continue working until I got to the panel that I would need to notch out for the outlet. That was a lot of slow cutting with a saw and utility knife. By the time

I got that piece cut and nailed to the wall, I was back heading in to take another hot shower. Convinced to just buckle down and finish this project, I went right back to work. I knew this pain. I knew exactly what it was.

Unfortunately, the outlet landed on a splice, so I had to notch out the next panel for the top of the outlet to fit. More slow cutting and utility knife work. This time when I went to nail it up, instead of heading for the shower, I just sat on the toilet seat and worked on my breathing. I was trying to stop or ease the pain before it really came on strong. I avoided another shower. I was able to make the sitting and resting work to ease the pain. I figured that we were running out of hot water anyways by now, as our dishwasher and washing machine are running all the time, as well, and who-knows-who else took a shower that morning.

Halfway done with the install and I'm at two showers and a rest stop. Over the next nine to ten panels to finish the job, I took at least two more hot showers and probably sat on the toilet resting another four or five times. I was finally done. I took everything out of the bathroom that I was using from the garage. With everything piled in the garage, I felt it coming again, so I left the pile and went in and laid down.

The pain subsided and it turned out to be one of the least painful ones that I had all day. My first thought was that maybe I just overdid it, especially after thinking I tweaked something Thursday night playing basketball with the boys. I don't do this often but convinced myself that the rest of the afternoon was going to be just hanging around and doing nothing.

As usual, that didn't last long. I had been hungry for chili for weeks, so by midafternoon I was up frying up pork and mixing all the ingredients in a kettle in order to have the chili ready by suppertime. I was trying to get it done by four-thirty because Jaicee had to work at five o'clock at her pizza market job. She was able to have a bowl and even though it was early, the boys and I ended up eating with her. Jaicee left for work and Jen joined us eating, as well. I don't make chili often and even though I try to watch the quantity of food I eat, when it comes to my chili, I usually eat too much.

After supper, we all cleaned up and I was ready to crash for the rest of the evening.

This day was also the day that all city league baseball and softball registrations were due in. Those come into a P.O. box at the post office and every day for about two months, I stop in at the post office and pick up any registrations that come in. Today was the last day and we could close the books.

I drove down to the post office and upon walking into the mailbox area, I could feel the pain going up my neck again. What? I really hadn't done anything since putting the tools away. I was extra careful on my movements and yet it was still coming on. I grabbed the mail that we had in the box and walked out to get into the van. Once I got in the van, I grabbed my phone first and since I didn't understand why this pain kept coming back, I looked up the symptoms of a heart attack. I did this same lookup two years ago though, so I already knew the answer. I read the symptoms were tiredness, dizziness, blurred vision and I didn't read any further. I wasn't tired or any more tired than I ever am. My vision was fine, and I didn't show any symptoms of dizziness. I think this was a check to tell myself I wasn't having a heart attack, rather than checking to see if I was.

The two-minute drive home was almost unbearable. I ran into the house almost in tears and headed straight for the shower. I could tell already when I turned the shower on that I had to turn it more to the hot side than normal when it started, as I'm assuming, we were still low on hot water. The pain did not subside. This was now the worst pain that I have ever had in anything that I've been a part of. The water was slowly turning colder, and I kept adjusting the dial, knowing it would soon come to an end.

We have a large five foot by six foot walk-in shower. I tried lying down on the floor to see if that helped my back. The problem was that by the time the water got down that far, it wasn't warm anymore. Standing up kept me closest to the nozzle, which means closest to the warmest water I was going to get that was coming out. I put my head against the side wall and turned the nozzle to hit the back of the neck as directly as possible.

It was at this time, that I realized something was different and something was wrong. My right arm or fingers weren't tingly or numb. They're always numb just like the left arm. The minute I noticed that, I yelled for Jen to call for an ambulance. Obviously, that is not something Jen was prepared to be asked and didn't know why. I was trying to explain to her that something wasn't right. I remember asking her how much it would cost to take the ambulance, but she convinced me that it didn't matter the cost and got on the phone, trying to get ahold of an ambulance to come.

The water was now cold. I knew I had to get out. The pain was still as intense as when I got in the shower, probably fifteen minutes earlier. I was able to barely dry off enough to be considered dried off. I slipped on my underwear and made my way to our walk-in closet. Our closet doubles as our main laundry area as well, so it's a pretty big area. All I could think of doing was lying on the floor.

I don't remember if I grabbed a pair of shorts or if Jen grabbed a pair for me. My first thought was, *Should I really wear my favorite Jordan shorts*, but that was a quick thought, because I was soon back to rolling back and forth on the closet floor to try to ease the pain. The pain now was mostly in my neck, my entire chest and my entire left arm. I've never hurt so bad in my entire life.

What seemed like a ton of time, was only a couple of minutes when I heard some familiar, friendly voices of some first responders that are friends of ours that only live a minute or two away. Though I may not have been the friendliest to them, I do remember the soothing voice of one that was doing whatever she could to help me catch my breath. I think just the fact they were there, put me a little more at ease that I was with people that could help do something. I remember a good amount of questions being asked, but I don't remember answering them. I was wearing two bracelets for people in town that have been going through medical issues, and as she was trying to pull them off gently, I remember telling her to just pull them off. She didn't want to pull my arm hair, but at this point, that pain would've meant nothing.

I continued to roll back and forth on the floor, begging for something to ease the pain. First responders don't have anything for the pain. It wasn't, but it seemed like it was another eternity, before I heard the voices of more medical staff coming into the closet. They had a stretcher with them and were going to lift me up into it. For an extremely odd reason, I felt a break coming in the onslaught of pain and I asked for them to wait a minute. I was helped to a sitting position and while two of them each had one of my hands, I gave them the go-ahead to help pull me up and got on the stretcher on my own. I don't remember anything else until I got outside.

While this was going on, my wife had instructed my sons to go to the basement. They were thinking all of this was for my bad neck, but it was still good for them not to see their dad on a stretcher getting wheeled out of the house.

The only other thing I remember before getting into the ambulance was going out the front door. The sun hit my eyes hard and I took one of my arms up over my face to block out the light that was shining in my eyes. I remember cold, as I was only wearing underwear and a pair of shorts. I remember the combination of bright light and the deep cold.

*****

Now I'm in the ambulance sitting in my driveway. I was begging for anything I could take for the pain. I don't know if they didn't have pain medicine or if they needed to wait until they did some tests to give me that pain medicine. I've been through similar situations with my gallbladder that they didn't want to give anything until they knew what they were dealing with. They said they were waiting for another ambulance to meet up with, in order to get some of their pain medicine for me. I think we were going to wait for them in my driveway, but then I heard someone suggest waiting for them on the interstate, off-ramp on the north side of town. We were heading that way anyway to get to the emergency room.

Jen told me later that this ambulance, which is from a town six miles west of us, was just passing by our town from another run they had just finished up on, when they got the call for me. From the time she called 911 to the time the ambulance pulled out of the driveway, she said it was almost exactly twenty minutes. If they wouldn't have been passing through, it would've been at least another ten minutes. These are all volunteer EMTs and first responders, so if they weren't at the fire station when they got the call, it could've taken much more time for them to get loaded and get to our house. Whether they had pain medicine for me or not, I'm thankful that they just happened to be on the highway coming up to our exit and saved us probably a half of hour or more.

We pulled out of the driveway. Jen was still thinking this was a spinal cord issue. I knew it was something more than that by now. Later, Jen told me that she was relieved because when the ambulance pulled out, they didn't turn their sirens on.

Right after I left, Jen called my daughter who was still working at her pizza market job in the center of town. She wanted Jaicee aware that something happened. With all the people that stop into the pizza shop, she didn't want Jaicee to hear about it from someone else. As they were chatting on the phone, Jen could hear the ambulance sirens go down main street over the phone.

I don't know if we stopped on the on-ramp or not to wait for another ambulance. In a short manner of time, the pain was starting to go away. I remember getting sleepy. I could hardly keep my eyes open and I remember them telling me I needed to keep them open. At times, the guy near my head would give me a little poke in the face to wake me up. I was at ease for the first time in what seemed like hours of pain. What I always imagined or seen in a movie was utter inorganization in the back of an ambulance. I remember for a brief couple of seconds thinking that this was extremely controlled and professional chaos. Nobody panicked. Everyone was doing their job. It seemed like they were working together on their own.

Then I heard a pair of scissors. When nothing else could hardly keep my eyes open, I heard that pair of scissors. I remember picking my head off the bed and seeing the guy by my feet with the pair of scissors. As I saw him cut up the left side of my favorite pair of Jordan shorts that

I wasn't thinking I should wear to begin with, I was a little in disbelief. He cut that entire left side of my shorts and underwear. By the time he got to the right side, I just put my head down and thought to myself, "*Dude, why didn't you just pull them off? I'm going to be naked either way but you could've saved the shorts.*"

I put my head down and closed my eyes. I don't remember them telling me to open them anymore on the ride. I don't remember the rest of the ride until they opened the back of the ambulance when I arrived at the hospital. The air was still cold. I was now wearing no clothes and only had this little thin sheet over the top of me. I now heard nothing.

*****

Bright lights again. I found myself in a room in the hospital. It felt like there were at least a dozen people in this small room. I remember thinking as I'm watching them, *How aren't they running into each other?* Only one guy seemed to be talking and everyone else was doing their responsibility on their own. I remember my eyes scanning the room and my ears listening intently to try to figure out what was going on. I expected way more chaos. The time had come for me to get off the stretcher and into my bed. Seemed like an army of people that lifted a blanket under me and got me over to the bed. Questions. Questions. Questions. I don't remember what they were. I don't remember the importance of them. I just remember questions and my eyes continuing to scan all the faces in the room. I'm assuming it is hard for medical staff to get started on stuff if they don't know much about me and if Jen isn't there to talk or answer the questions for me.

Oxygen mask went on which ruined my visibility of what was going on in the room. I didn't have any more pain. I felt, again, at ease and in good hands. That amazing chili supper that I made for my family just hours ago, physically revisited my life and showed the medical staff at least what I had for supper that night. Unfortunately, I still had my oxygen mask on when that started, so that creates other complications that I would find out about later.

The last thing I heard was, "Looks like we had a chili supper." I was out.

*****

In the meantime, back home, Jen was still under the impression that this was a spinal cord issue. After about an hour, Jen looked up a number for the emergency room and thought she should call in to see how I was doing. She was told that it wasn't a spinal cord issue, and it had been listed as a cardiac issue. They switched her over to a supervisor. The supervisor got on the phone and apologized for having to tell her this way, but she needed to come to the hospital quickly. She had to come alone. She was told that they have already resuscitated me twice and it wasn't looking good moving forward. I found out months later that one of the times they lost me, I was out for nearly two minutes, and they needed to use an electronic defibrillator multiple times to bring me back. If that does not hit you hard, I do not know what will.

I would assume this was a case of shock for Jen. What seemed like old news with the neck, now turned into things weren't good and I might not make it. Jen got ready and was starting to leave. Our boys were home alone, and even though they do that all the time, this was different. She tried to get ahold of her mother, and she was going to come, but it would be another twenty minutes. With social distancing in full effect for the coronavirus, it made it difficult for her to ask anyone else. Jen left. While driving through town, she pulled into the pizza shop to let Jaicee know briefly what was going on. She just wanted to talk to Jaicee's boss and explain things and have her send Jaicee home, but Jaicee and her boss both met Jen by the front counter. Jen suggested to Jaicee that she needs to go home and be with her brothers, as she needed to run to the emergency room to see me.

After Jaicee turned away to get her things and leave, Jen was able to let our friend that owns the pizza place know that things weren't good, and we appreciate her understanding, the need of letting Jaicee leave work early. Jaicee went home. In the meantime, another set of friends heard about what was going on somehow and came over to check on the kids. Grandma was here watching the kids in a short amount of time, as well. I don't know if I was told the full timeline of everything, which really doesn't matter. I'm sure for Jen and everyone else involved, time stood still and was flying by all at the same time.

Jen arrived at the hospital. She was still confused and not understanding what was going on. When she got into the front doors, she had to go through the coronavirus protocol to go any further. She then got escorted through the basement to a secluded waiting room and was given a phone number to call if she didn't hear from anyone in the next twenty minutes.

After a few minutes, a chaplain appeared and asked Jen if she could tell her what had happened. Jen told her everything she knew to this point and then was asked to pray with the chaplain. She accepted and though confused about what they were really praying for yet, enjoyed the time of being with someone in the basement of the hospital.

After another twenty to thirty minutes, Jen called the number that they told her to call. They now told her that she needed to move to another waiting room. The chaplain agreed to take her to the new waiting room. Since most of the time the hallways of the basement are not used, Jen seemed to think that the chaplain didn't know exactly where she was going.

After some time walking around in the halls, they came to another room and this is where the chaplain was confident that Jen had to be. With nobody around and nobody walking the halls, Jen sat in this waiting room for another hour. Afraid that she was in the wrong waiting room and that nobody would know where she was, she finally got ahold of someone that confirmed she was in the right spot. They told her that they were finishing up on some stuff with me and that it wouldn't be much longer.

This whole time, she didn't see anyone. She was now up in the hospital for over two hours and knew nothing and only had conversations with the chaplain that came to visit with her.

They eventually came and got her. Walking my way and heading to my room, Jen didn't know what to expect. Her thoughts were that she was going to walk into my room, see me and the doctor sitting there, and he was going to tell her that her husband is okay, and needs to take it easy. She was expecting to walk in, talk a little bit, and then take me home to rest.

Instead, she walked into a room where I was in a hospital bed. Tubes and cords were coming out any place a tube or cord can be and then some. She was told that it did not appear that I had any brain damage that they could see. They explained that I was responsive to their questions and would react as they were hoping I would. So instead of getting the "take it easy" message from the doctor, she had to see me in this way with no preparation to take it in. I'm guessing she was probably in shock now again.

She asked them what they meant by brain issues and responsiveness of me. She doesn't even know what happened yet. She asked the person she was with to slow down and explain this all again and what was going on.

The doctor then came in and was trying to explain again to Jen what was happening. Jen also told him to stop, slow down, and re-explain what is going on. She just had two plus hours of sitting alone in secluded waiting rooms getting little to no information from anyone during that time. I'm assuming and picturing this to be almost like a horror movie for her. Anyone expecting to walk into a room to sit next to and hug their spouse, only to see them in a position that I was in, can only put someone into a state of shock or confusion.

They explained what was going on. They explained to her why my arms were tied down to the bed. This is so when I wake up, I wouldn't panic and try ripping the tube out of the throat. They told her that I could hear her and respond to her if she wanted to talk to me. If she said anything to me, I don't remember it at all, and I was not awake.

Jen ended up sitting in the room for a while but felt extremely helpless. She then decided to leave and go home to be with the kids and send Grandma back home. Our friends that stopped in to check on the kids said they were expecting to walk into the front door in a position of consoling our kids when they got here. They apparently walked in the front door to the kids playing and laughing and being themselves. Jen didn't share details with the kids at all, but our friends didn't know that. They said they had to pull themselves together while walking in, especially when they saw the kids were handling everything so well.

Jen got home and put her mom in charge of contacting and communicating what she knew to her side of the family. She also got ahold of my mom to reach out to everyone on my side of the family. I'm so proud of Jen for doing this, as this can be the most daunting task of any situation if you think you need to communicate with everyone on your own. This also kept many phone calls, emails and texts off Jen's plate, so she could take some alone time to figure things out.

Q usually takes any opportunity, when I'm traveling for work and not home at night, to get Jen to sleep with him. He, of course, asked this time, as well. Jen told him no but would the next night. After the kids were in bed, Jen had a long night ahead of her. She couldn't sleep at all. The bed was empty. With every car that drove past our house, she was woken up, wondering if it was a patrol car that was stopping to knock on the door and tell her the bad news that I didn't make it. I can't imagine that feeling while attempting to get any sleep on what she probably thought was going to be a long couple of weeks coming up.

*****

Sunday morning, I woke up to a roomful of doctors and nurses. I don't know if I woke up on my own, but I'm assuming they woke me up since everyone was in there. I remember them asking me some questions, but as I tried to respond, they told me that I wasn't able to talk. Already I was back enough to question why I'm being asked questions that I can't answer. They untied my arms from the bed. I lifted my right arm in the air and waved my hand around in a manner that I was holding a pen and wanted to write. They got me a note pad and marker and asked me some questions again. Still don't remember the questions, but I do remember answering them by writing out the answers. That seemed to impress the doctor.

Shortly after the doctor left the room, they removed the tube from my throat. First time with that in for me. Wow is all I'm going to say to that. They took my vitals and started me on some of the medication that I will need to take for some time now.

I ended up falling back to sleep for a couple hours until I awoke again for vital checks. Shortly after this, my catheter got taken out. That trumped the wow of the throat tube, as that was my first time with one of those in as well. Wasn't painful, just unique. The nice thing about this was that I was up on my feet when this got removed. It felt so good to be standing.

By noon, I was walking the halls with my nurse. Still hooked-up to machines, I was able to pull those along with me and do circles around the ICU. I'm almost walking around feeling like I'm good to go. I still wasn't told anything. I still didn't know how bad things had been. I still hadn't talked to Jen. All I knew was that most of the pain was gone and I was on my feet again. The only pain I still had was an extremely sore left arm and a sore chest. I didn't know why though, and honestly didn't care at that moment. I was just happy to be walking around.

I got back to the room and decided to order myself some food. I was told that because I had a heart attack that I need to only order items that had a heart next to them on the menu. Then it sunk in. I had a heart attack. I remember looking that up at the post office and telling myself again that I can't believe it was a heart attack. My enthusiasm for being able to walk around in the hallways came down a couple of notches. I wasn't getting out of here anytime soon and the reality of not being able to see Jen or the kids until I got home had now sunk in.

I ordered my food (just grapes, pudding, and sherbet) and just as I was about to call Jen, the doctor came back in. He was extremely shocked that I was sitting up in bed watching television and was even more surprised when he heard I was out walking for twenty minutes already earlier that morning. He reminded me to take it easy, but to continue to get exercise as I could without overdoing it.

With the phone still in hand, I finally got a chance to call Jen. It was a hard phone call. Just hearing the news, myself about having a heart attack, I couldn't imagine what she had went through while I was going through everything unknowingly. It was so good to hear her voice. She was with the kids as I believe they were also eating together at home. We talked for a minute or two. It was hard between the emotions, the sore throat, the coughing from aspiration pneumonia, and the tight pain in my chest. I don't know that I talked too much, as that call was a blur. Everything flashed before my eyes and I started to remember the night before. She asked if I wanted to talk to each of the kids and though I did, I said no. She then explained to them that I couldn't talk well, so she put me on speaker phone and let them each say hi to me. It was great to hear their voice but hard, as I was assuming, it would still be a while before I saw them.

Jen came back on the phone and we talked a little more. Emotions were starting to run high, so I had to end the call. I knew she had enough going on at home and didn't want her worried about my emotional state too.

By now, she was getting hit hard with phone calls, emails, and texts. We have a great family and super friends. Because of my coaching and involvement with youth sports and activities in town, we've gotten to know a lot of people who have become great friends of ours over the years. Some friends put together a meal schedule that some of them were going to work on to make sure Jen and the kids didn't have to worry about meals while I was gone.

The prayers, concerns, and love that were pouring in were, I'm sure, overwhelming to Jen, but as strong as she is, she did her best to respond to everyone and keep all those reaching in, in the loop about how things were. Though they are friends and neighbors, we really consider all these people our family. She continued to update our moms on how things were going, so they could work on communicating as needed with the siblings. She must have had a system to make sure everything was done, as I don't think she missed anyone that reached out to her. There were several more people that I think she wanted to reach out to but had all she could handle keeping up with everything else. So thankful for the support. With the support that we got knowing I was going to make it; I can only imagine the support Jen and the kids would've gotten if I wouldn't have.

By midafternoon, I was on my second walk with my nurse. It felt so good to get out of bed and walk around. I had great nurses that were patient, gentle, and didn't mind how long I walked. They had to be there with me, and they just kept doing circles around the hallway with me.

I called Jen later that night and talked for a little bit. While we were talking, she asked if I knew what happened. I told her yes, even though I didn't know the whole story.

She asked if I wanted to talk about it and I said no. I did. I didn't. I just wanted to hear her voice. I don't think I talked to the kids that night, it was just a short call to say hi and good night.

By the end of the evening, I was removed from having anyone help me go the bathroom or from walking the halls. I was somewhat free to move around my room as needed and could come in and out of my room as I liked if I stayed in the designated area in the ICU. It was nice to not have to rely on anyone.

I got very little sleep that night. Nurses turned my lights down but not off. I assumed they needed them on a little for all the times they were going to come in through the night. One of the nurses in the ICU had a voice that pierced through the door, a little more than others. Once I heard it, I couldn't unhear it. That kept me up some. Pillows weren't comfortable. Bed wasn't long enough for the legs to stay straight. I'm more of a stomach sleeper and now had to be on my back. My left arm and chest still hurt a lot, but they said that was normal. I woke up around two o'clock and watched television for maybe an hour and went back to sleep.

*****

Though I didn't get much sleep during the night, I woke up feeling pretty good. I ended up ordering my first full meal shortly after I woke up. I didn't know if I could have milk, so I ordered dry Rice Chex with some cut fruit and of course, more vanilla pudding and sherbet. My throat was still a little tender and most of this was easy on that. Fruit was horrible because it seemed like it had been cut up two days prior and had that nasty coating over it.

I did wake up Monday morning for the first time with no pain in my left arm. Chest still hurt when I coughed or hacked something up. I could tell that was slowly starting to get better as well though.

This morning also brought with it a new nurse that I hadn't had yet. She was nice. Turned out she knew a family that I am friends with in town. That gave us something to talk about. I found out very quickly that she was a person of faith, as she discussed some of the concerts that she's been to and one that was recently cancelled because of the coronavirus. We ended up getting into a conversation about what God does for us and how he is in our lives even when things aren't going well. It was great timing for me because I was feeling like it was almost time for me to leave, yet most were telling me already that it would be at least one more night. The television was keeping me the most occupied and this was a nice break and reminder that broke up the long day that was about to come.

The nurse asked what I was going to do with my second chance at life. Is that a question or comment that everyone is going to say now? I had a heart attack and it was scary, I'm sure, for everyone, but I didn't die. I understand the comments *second chance at life*, but I guess I wasn't sure how that applied to me.

After our long conversation about Christian concerts, the Kirk Cameron Event that Jen and I just went to, me and my daughter's trip to Lifest last year, and the mission trips that the nurse and Jen and Jaicee took the last couple of years; the rest of the day was pretty quiet and boring. After probably ten full episodes of the antique show, American Pickers, that I had watched on and off, and several walks alone around the ICU desk area, it was a long day.

I was able to talk to Jen and the kids a couple of times on this day. This was the first time that I talked to each of the kids separately. The boys were their typical selves. Quillan probably was telling me something about sports or what he was doing with basketball outside. Jorey gave me a rundown of all the meals that different families dropped off for them. I don't want to take anything away from the love I have for my boys, but I was and wasn't looking forward to my next conversation that was still coming. For any of you guys that have a daughter, there is just something different about that relationship over any relationship you'll ever have with anyone else. I was happy to hear that she was spending most of her days upstairs with Jen and the boys, as she's usually busy with homework and stays in her room most of the time.

It was time to talk to Jaicee though, and hearing her voice was emotional. I tried hard to keep it together and be strong. I didn't know what they knew or didn't know. I honestly don't remember what she told me. I was just listening to her voice. I was sitting in a chair in the room, looking out a window to an interior hallway and probably was just off in a daze. I had several quick thoughts flash through my head, such as a missed graduation, me missing her college experience, and missing walking her down the aisle. I knew with any heart attack, there's always a risk that you might not come out of that and survive. I ended the phone call with hardly being able to say, "I love you and goodbye." I think I hung up kind of quickly.

Shortly after this, I got introduced to my new male nurse. He was a great guy and very easy to talk to and communicate with. Right out of the gate, he mentioned that I looked way better than I did the night I came in. He said he was working that night but wasn't with me. He would now be my nurse tonight through tomorrow morning when the shift changes again.

He was a great nurse; I could tell already—very engaging and explaining everything he was doing and why. By now though, I was up and out of my bed often. Whether that meant sitting in the different chairs in the room, walking around the room, or going for walks in the hallway.

The first time he came in to do my vitals on his own, he asked me if anyone told me anything about Saturday night. I told him I knew a little, but most of that was from what I remembered on my own. Jen and I still didn't talk about anything and I really assumed that there wasn't much more.

He asked if I wanted to know everything. Did I? Emotions were all over the place yet from talking with Jaicee and the boys. So, he asked me what I remembered and just sat there and listened to my story. I guess I probably started with everything that happened at the house and went into the ambulance ride, as well. He again asked if I wanted to know more and when I agreed to hear it, he went on to tell me all the things that I didn't know.

He told me that Saturday night was bad. This was the first time that someone had told me that the doctors had lost me twice and resuscitated me both times. They struggled both times to keep me alive. I told him I needed a second to let that soak in and my mind immediately went to Jen. What had she gone through? What did she know? Is she still scared? I can say all I want about how I feel over the phone, but she hasn't seen me in over two days, and I didn't know that she was at the hospital at all the first night. I was thinking about how most people only get one change at life and thirty seconds into my conversation with my nurse, I felt like I was on life number three already. This explained the comments about what I'm going to do with my extra opportunities with life.

The nurse touched my arm and asked if I needed more time. It seemed like ten minutes of sitting there, trying to soak it all in, but I'm assuming it was only a couple of seconds. He asked if I remember throwing up, which was one of the last things that I had remembered. He said that one of the pills I was taking was to help me with aspiration pneumonia because I breathed in some of my vomit. He asked if I wanted to hear the rest or just leave it alone. By now, I wanted to hear it all. I wanted it thrown straight at me so I could absorb it and move on.

He went on to tell me that how I was when I came in and with the procedures that had been done on me, that my chances of making it through Saturday night were around four percent. With that four percent, ninety percent of the time, the person wakes up with some sort of defects or a change to how they used to be—that might be memory loss or lack of use in some limbs or brain not working as it normally would. Whew! That was tough to soak in. I told him I needed a minute to soak that all in, too. I started to think, *Am I back to the way I was before I went in. I felt fine. I seemed like I remembered things. Is my brain working the way it is supposed to and do I even know how it is supposed to? I really felt fine.* After wiping the tears away, I asked him where he thought I was. He told me that he is so amazed that I beat the four percent odds and don't seem to have any lingering effects that most people have after this.

He left the room and I was able to call Jen and talk for a while. At this time, I guess I was still hopeful that I could go home that night, even though it was obvious I was staying for another night. I asked Jen if she knew that information that I was just told. She knew it was bad and she knew how lucky I was. It was a short call as the doctor was waiting outside the door to talk with me. The doctor told me that I was going to stay another night, but based on how I was doing, she thought I would be released by eleven o'clock the next morning.

I went for a walk in the hallways after this. I could tell that the rooms were filling up more and they had mentioned that they may have to move me to another room if too many more people came in that night. I was hoping I could just stay where I was at with the nurses that I had.

The nurses were suggesting that I should probably take a shower that night. I really wasn't looking forward to going through all that until they told me there was a shower room in the corner and that I was probably good enough to take my own shower without help. It sounded great then, but we'd see how much I would be able to do on my own once it got started.

They showed me where to go and they set up everything in the room for me. I really didn't believe they would end up letting me do this on my own, but I was wrong. They told me that I could pull off all the sensors that were stuck all over my chest and stomach. I had to get all the IVs wrapped in plastic on both arms, so those didn't get wet. This was also the first time that I was able to look in a mirror since I was there.

As I was getting undressed, I noticed that my chest was all yellow. I asked the nurse what that was, and she told me it was probably bruising from several broken ribs I got from the CPR that was performed. I guess that made sense. This was the first time that I put CPR together with resuscitation, and then how brutal that probably is on anyone's ribs. I'll take broken ribs over the alternative I had any day.

The shower felt great. For a very quick moment, I looked back and remembered this is where it all kind of started. The hot water felt so good. This trumped the peeling-off of the tape and sensors that were on my body. Things were going slow, but I didn't care. Other than a couple check-ins from the nurse, I was left alone and under hot water. Took probably ten minutes to get everything off as needed. The next thirty minutes were all mine. Washed and shampooed everything once through and then just stood under the water. Went to turn the water off and decided to wash and shampoo everything for a second time. I didn't want to leave the shower, but I figured if I didn't, someone would come in and get me out.

After drying off and putting on pants that Jen dropped off, I went back to my room and was just going to settle in and hopefully get some better sleep tonight. The nurse came in to reapply new censors all over my chest and stomach to the replace the ones I had just painfully ripped off my body.

After my vitals and medicines were all taken, the nurse turned around to leave. I probably wouldn't see him for a couple more hours until he came in through the night to check my vitals again. He asked if I wanted the lights off, and I told him that would've been nice last night. Lights got turned all the way off and I was prepping myself to try to get a good night's sleep. As he was closing the door behind him when he walked out, he turned and said to me, "You're alive, you're moving around, you're eating and communicating like nothing happened…you must be on the good side of the guy upstairs who obviously loves you and has more plans for you."

What do you do with that comment, just minutes before you are trying to get some needed sleep? I laid there for a while and thought about those words. God loves me the same as he loves everyone else. I love him and appreciate everything he has ever done for me. I believe that he created us. I believe that he sent his son to die for us. I believe that Jesus will come again, and we will all be judged on that last day. He has plans for all of us. It was a lot to think about and I was exhausted and finally fell asleep.

*****

I got a pretty good sleep that night. I was up and at it early that morning. I ordered my breakfast right away and went for a walk in the hallway. I was kind of hoping to be walking around when the doctor that would eventually release me walked in. At about seven o'clock, there was a shift change. This would probably be the last time I had the nurse that told me everything. The night shift and the new shift were all coming together to go over everything together, in the middle of where I was walking.

My nurse introduced me to my new nurse, who I immediately told would only have me for a couple hours. She seemed nice and I went about working on that walk to impress the doctor when he arrived. My next lap around the room, I heard my nurse tell the new nurse a little bit about what I went through, and she just blurted out, "That's the guy?" She mentioned that she did not even think I would be out of bed yet and here I am walking around getting ready to go home. She typically worked in a different department but had heard about me from others.

He mentioned to her that it has been pretty amazing how quickly I've been able to get up and about and that I'm an easy patient.

Tired of walking and still not seeing my doctor, I decided to stop. I got back in my room and my breakfast showed up within minutes. This morning I ordered eggs, or what were supposed to be eggs, along with my grapes and vanilla pudding. I gagged down this egg-like substance and instantly didn't feel the best.

The nurses meeting broke-up and within minutes, my old nurse came in to say goodbye. He was on his way out while my new nurse was coming in. He told her that I was like a superhero based on what I had gone through. He did kind of make me feel superhuman at times in the way he detailed the story.

The new nurse wanted details. She said that she needed to hear everything that happened because she couldn't believe it. I took my breakfast tray and gathered everything together to clean up that area. She asked what I had for breakfast and said hopefully I didn't have the eggs. I told her I had the eggs and they really weren't making me feel very good. Didn't matter though, because she wanted the story before anything else. After I got done telling her everything that I knew, she just stood in front of me with a look of *are you kidding me* on her face. I just told her that's it.

After a bit of awkward silence, she started asking me a bunch of questions. She discussed that she's always worried about that happening to her and didn't know what she would do with her kids even though they were a little older than mine are. I don't remember her exact words, but she said something like, "Isn't God great? What a great opportunity you have to do something with your new chance on life." Again, what do you do with that? God is great. Why do we need to do something special on our second chance at life? I feel like I try to do those things all the time, regardless of what life I'm on.

After what seemed to be an extremely long morning, I saw the two doctors that would need to release me walking around in the hallway. I got up from my chair and started walking around the room. I really wanted them to know that I was working hard at moving around and building up my strength again. Even though the nurses said I was probably going home, I wanted to make it definite that I was.

They walked in my room and looked at each other. The head one turned to me and said, "It sounds and appears like you're ready to go."

I told him that it's obviously his choice, but I feel like the time is right for me to go and I've been feeling good. He released me and got my pharmacy prescription ordered for me to pick up after I got picked up.

I called Jen and let her know that I was released but still had a couple hours of going through stuff. I would call her back when I knew more of a time that I would be done.

Well, here I go, back to ripping off all the sensors on my chest and stomach. This time, I didn't have the hot water to ease the pain of ripping them off. Nurse had to rip off all the tape that was holding in my IVs and then pull them out. I had been wearing underwear and sweatpants for the last two days already, but when I reached in to grab the t-shirt that I was going to wear home, I noticed a couple of notes in there from the kids. This was the first time

I saw the notes and it was a great way to finalize my stay at the hospital. I called Jen and told her I would be down by the front doors in about twenty minutes and to meet me there. So just as I was ready to leave the room, I saw a bunch of blood on the floor, only to find out that one of my bandages from the IV being taken out was leaking and I was bleeding all over. I had a quick thought of, *Oh no, I'm not going to get to leave now.* We redid the bandage and cleaned everything up and I was still good to go as planned.

Since I did not wear anything to the emergency room, other than my now-ruined shorts and underwear, Jen only dropped off some underwear, sweatpants, and a t-shirt on the second day; I didn't have any shoes or jacket with me. With no shoes they decided to wheelchair me down to the front door, which was probably for the best. After twenty minutes, Jen still wasn't there. We went back into the hospital to call her because, thankfully, I didn't have my cellphone with me either. She mentioned she was about halfway there, so we went back to waiting by the front window like an old man in a wheelchair.

Finally saw Jen's van coming around the corner. She pulled the van up by the door and got out to come put my shoes and jacket on. It was so great to see her. It had been so long. After she slipped my shoes on and helped me get my jacket on, we just stood there and hugged. I felt like I could've stood there all day.

It was nice to just sit and listen to her talk while we headed to pick up all my new prescriptions. Having to go through the pharmacy drive-through, they told us the prescriptions weren't going to be filled for another forty-five minutes, so we just pulled into a stall to talk and wait. This is when she filled me in on the first night that she had and the surprise she had when she walked into my room that night. She went through all the people that had reached out to her and kept all the text messages and read them to me while we waited. We are truly blessed to have the people we have in our lives. I was overwhelmed with all the support that Jen and the kids had while I was not able to support them myself.

Well, this was a long wait yet. The eggs started to kick in a little more than I felt comfortable sitting in the van for. I decided I better go use the restroom of the pharmacy, only to arrive to the only stall to find a guy sitting in there. For another ten minutes, I staggered around the pharmacy, trying to make it seem like I wasn't stealing something or waiting to use the bathroom. After about fifteen minutes, the guy that was sitting on the toilet with his phone came out and went into the employee breakroom. Seems like someone was just on break and needed some alone time. Glad I could wait that one out for him.

Got back to the van and went back in line to pick up the prescriptions in the drive-through. There was a lot of prescriptions and the pharmacist had to go through each one with us. We were finally on our way home and I was going to be able to see the kids again. The ride home was quick. We pulled into the garage and I just sat there. This was going to be emotional. Jen told me that she really didn't tell them much and that maybe we should wait to give them any details. I sat there a little longer, got a hug from Jen, and decided it was time to go in and face the kids.

Q was the first one to meet me. He gave me a quick hug and said he missed me and took off downstairs to finish the video game that he was playing. The other two were sitting in the living room waiting for me. After a hug from each of them, I sat down in our chair, we call our reading chair. The four of us talked a little bit and Jen thought it was a good idea for Jorey to show me one of his new card tricks he was working on. I agreed that this would be good and as he started, I got to a point that I could not watch. Not that the trick was bad, I just saw him trying so hard but struggling a little to make it work the exact way he wanted to. He's a lot like me in that way. I buried my head in my hands and was the most emotional I've been during this whole time.

I lifted my head and turned to Jen and she said, "Go ahead." I went on to tell Jaicee and Jorey what happened, what I went through, and that twice, the doctors had to bring me back to life. We were planning on telling them later, but I wanted them to hear it from me and I wanted that off my chest now. We've decided to not tell Q yet. I can tell this information changed them. All of my kids now need to be aware of this as they get older because this incident was mostly hereditary.

Recovery is now in full effect. We've been able to eat meals together, as the kids are on spring break this week from the coronavirus quarantined homeschooling. We've been able to play games together, watch movies together, and just spend quality time with each other that many times we've taken for granted.

*****

Now what? I do the walks I'm supposed to do each day. Actually, I have been walking twice as far as what I'm supposed to. I take my pills religiously, probably because I was told I better not miss a couple of them. I'm eating all the bland, tasteless food that I possibly can. I do miss my spicy stuff already, but this is what the next chapter of my life will be like moving forward.

What about all these questions I was asked about the next opportunities this new chance on life was going to give me? Is God expecting something in return from me? I owe him everything, but he also has everything already. Is there something for me to do? My head keeps wrapping around the fact that I need to do something. Is this common? Does everyone feel like this after they go through a dramatic situation like this?

Even though I joked about the bland food that I now eat, it is something that I must do. I do not necessarily like it, but it is part of my life now. Is taking-it-easy going to have to be a part of my life and for how long?

The problem with all these questions is that nobody has an answer other than our Lord and Savior, Jesus Christ. He doesn't always answer right away. He doesn't always answer us in a way that we can clearly understand what he is saying. He doesn't answer us with the answer we wanted to hear to begin with.

There is prayer—that just sits and stares me in the face now every day. Prayer. I can honestly say that I've always questioned the power of prayer. We say the Lord's Prayer in church every week, but are we are saying it or are we reciting it? To me, there is a big difference between the two. And not just the Lord's Prayer, what else are we just reciting along to while at church. I think there are many times that you get done with those things and not even realize you participated and after the service is done, tell yourself that Pastor must have forgotten to do that today, even though we did it.

We pray before each meal that we eat together at home. When we have lunch at our parent's, we say a similar prayer before we eat, but each family says it a little different. We'll be eating at times and one of the kids will say, "Shouldn't we pray?" after we just got done praying. Again, are we praying or reciting something that we could all say in our sleep. What meaning does it have if we are just saying it to say it?

I don't put Q to bed often, as he normally votes for Jen to do that. The other two go to bed on their own and should be praying to themselves before they go to bed. When I pray with Q, it's usually just a short, recited prayer that we've all done since we were kids. Do the other two pray at all? I didn't, when I was their age. We stopped doing family night prayers when I was probably in sixth grade. Do they need to pray if it doesn't mean anything to them?

I feel like we're in a rut right now when it comes to prayer. And then a situation comes up like this and I can honestly say that the strength of prayer from many family and friends got me through that first night at the hospital. There is no other way, because I wasn't supposed to make it that night. Even though I did make it, I wasn't supposed to come out as the same person I was before this all started. I question table prayer. I question church prayer. I question night prayer. Yet, there is no questioning the power of prayer when it is done honestly for the intent of talking one-on-one with God himself. He answered the prayers of what seems to be from a lot of people. He's continuing to answer the prayers as I go through the recovery process. Though my ribs still hurt and the walking is slow, he's letting me know every day that I'm getting better.

I can't say that I'm going to become this rock star prayer artist. I can't say that I'm going to stop reciting the three prayers that we are accustomed to saying. I can say that when someone needs an extra prayer, I will come up with that in my own non-recited way. It's time for me to personalize my prayers and get involved spiritually when someone is in need.

I think I fall into the trap when someone is going through a tough time or the loss of a loved one, of saying,

"My thoughts and prayers are with you." I'm guilty of not following through on this. I can admit that I always do a little bit or say something to God like, "God, please be with them and get them through this." That's it. Feels like a one-and-done. When you aren't completely convinced on the power of prayer, you don't put everything into it. Does God just think you're going through the motions? Well he doesn't have to think, he already knows. Do going-through-the-motion prayers help anyone? Maybe, they do. Maybe God sees that we are taking time out of our busy schedule and at least, thinking or saying something. Maybe God is disappointed though, that we are only taking a second out of our busy schedule and not doing what we are supposed to do and what he has asked us to do.

Prayer. Thank you to everyone that showed me the purpose and power of prayer. I feel like a hypocrite waiting for something to happen to me, before I woke up to realize what God's expectations probably are when we need to talk to him. It's okay that he doesn't answer right away. It's his decision to not answer in a way that we were hoping it would go. And in all honesty, it's fine if he doesn't answer our prayers at all because of what he already gives us each day.

*****

Does God have a plan for me? Just me, specifically? Is it more than what I already do all the time? Does it take a near-fatal situation to determine that someone needs to do more? What if I'm already doing the plan and he just gave me more time to complete it? It would be a lot easier if we just knew the answers. We need to continue to talk and more importantly, listen to what God is telling us. He doesn't verbalize his answers. He doesn't send you an email asking you to help with something. He creates a situation that you need to have a deep relationship with him so you can feel what needs to be done.

There is a chance that I'm going down a wrong path or doing the wrong plan. If that is the case, I do feel that I will be redirected in some way. Though he's calling all the shots, he gives us some room to make the decisions that we feel are the right things to do. We will make mistakes. We will get lost at times. We will want to give-up. We will allow distractions to come into our lives. The key is to stay with it or get back to it, depending on where we are at with our journey.

The plan is already figured out for me and you. God knows what we will do with it. He knows how involved we will be and what priority it will be in our lives. Is it time to change our priorities? A heart attack, for me, has me deeply thinking about my priorities. Though he's always been in the top three, I need to make sure God stays at the top of the list permanently. At times he's slipped down the list because of Jen, or because of the kids. There have been times that on the top of the list came a baseball or basketball team at a moment. The priority I need to make and commit to first is that God needs to be a permanent number one in my life.

My permanent number two needs to be Jen. The sacrifices she makes already for me, to coach multiple teams every season, is probably too much for her. She takes care of all the kid's appointments, most of the meals, and most of the housework. Her part-time job is more of a full-time job, plus all these extra duties at home. Most nights, after my full-time job, I head right to the gym or practice field. Coaching multiple teams that are different ages might mean that I have back-to-back practices on the same night. After practice, I'll come home in what will be our third installation of supper that night. None of us eating together. Me finishing up with my meal, cleaning up, taking a shower, and heading to bed.

Just recently we started a few things for just the two of us that *forces* us to stay connected and working on this family as a team. We've designated times that we need to talk about our days and what is going on in our lives. We make sure that we sit down on Sunday evenings and discuss everything that is on the calendar for that upcoming week. We pick two nights a week to just shutting-everything-off and being together. Though I don't ever like talking about work, it's a good time for me to listen to her talk about her work. Rather than living by a dry erase board calendar by the back door, we discuss who is going to be where and how they are going to get there. We try to plan out meals for a week to make sure we have what is needed and we aren't scrambling at the last minute. Jen and I need to stay in communication mode. We need to do this together, and even when it seems like one of us may be doing most of the work, by communicating, it still shows that we are doing it together.

The kids need to round out my top three. Though our kids need Jen and I to support them and provide for them, they are still number three on the list. Things need to be good in the number one and two spots if this third spot will be able to work as well. Fortunately for us, our two oldest children are old enough and responsible enough to take care of a lot of their own things. Having a daughter that drives and can get herself to school or work or run her own errands is already a load off our schedule. Many parents wish the day never comes that their child gets their driver's license, but we've enjoyed every minute of it if she is careful and responsible.

Jorey can sit all day and read a book and when he is done, he'll grab another one and just keep going. He can entertain himself and goes about his own business with all the interests that he has.

Quillan on the other hand, can't sit for too long. He needs to be active and that usually means a ball in his hands.

Though he can be very good about doing that on his own, he still needs someone around most of the time to watch him, rebound for him, retrieve balls for him, or whatever else he talks us into doing. These things are at times overwhelming, but Jen and I try to take advantage of our time with him, as it won't be that way forever.

It almost sounds cruel to say that the people that need us most in their lives are third on our priority list. I firmly believe that this is what it needs to be. Jen and I need to communicate. We need to be on the same page. We need to have a consistent message to our kids. We need to show our kids that we put God first, spouse second, and the rest falls in after that.

After the third spot, I think, that is for the rest of the important people in our lives. That includes our extended family, our church family, our neighbors, our close friends, and anyone else that is an important positive influence on your life. To us, close friends and neighbors are family and we treat them as such, and they seem to do the same in return.

After this large group of people is when we fill it in with our activities, the running to baseball tournaments, the practices, the vacations, the celebrations and parties. This is where my priorities need to change. As mentioned, games and practices sometimes creep into the top three and that can't happen. It's a hard message to send though to kids that I'm coaching, as we want them all-in when we are at practice or starting to focus twenty minutes before a game. You want to teach them responsibility and respect for what they are about to do while not making it seem like the most important thing in their life. You want them to give it everything they have when they step on the field or court, but not above and beyond the more important things in life. I'm sure that was confusing to me growing up, and it probably has gotten no easier on kids today.

As we are amidst the coronavirus, I've read several things on Facebook about people frustrated on the things that they are missing out on. I feel for those people, especially the young people that worked hard to achieve something, only for it to be ended or pulled away from them. I know the amount of time I put into those activities when I was their age, so I feel their pain. Hearing others complain that they can't go to a restaurant they like or the bar they like to sit at isn't open right now really doesn't hurt my feelings. I feel for the owners of those places that have had to temporarily close, but if a restaurant or bar is that high on your priority list, then I think your priority list needs to be re-examined as well.

I rarely post on social media. I have a Facebook account, but unless it is a post about our baseball or basketball teams, I usually don't write anything. Maybe it was my emotions of dodging a bullet and not dying from the heart attack, or maybe it was just a greater appreciation for all the things that I have in my life, I nervously went to social media to send a message. Keep in mind that at this time, everyone is quarantined and are supposed to be taking part in social distancing. I only had two friends that work at the hospital stop and see me in the four days I was there. I have not seen my extended family at all on either side. I have not seen or talked to most of my friends, other than the ones I see from a distance on one of my strengthening walks. So, I had my phone in my hand. I had the ringing in my head of people telling me to tell my story. Others saying that my story might help someone else, and maybe that is my calling. I don't know what my calling is. I don't know if my experience is something that is part of my plan or even something worth sharing. Suddenly, I found myself writing. Here is the message I wrote…

I heard a very important message today listening to a streamed sermon this morning. The title was something like "Don't Waste This Quarantine." I know the pains, the loneliness, and the financial burdens that this has caused many people. But also, like many, I needed this quarantine. For those that don't know, last Saturday, I suffered a near-fatal heart attack and was in the ICU for four days. As painful as it was to not see Jen and the kids that entire time, I needed that quarantine time with no visitors to make sure I healed. I needed that time, when I finally came home as well, as it allowed me to spend time with just my family while in one of the lowest times in my life. This time with just family allowed for meals together, games and movies together, and just sitting and talking. I have never really been able to do all that consistently. Please don't misunderstand any of this. I get the burdens that this puts on life. I sincerely feel horrible for all our kids that are missing out on things they love and feel compassion for, anyone that is forced to be alone right now. I now understand though that this was something I needed and I'm not wasting this time. God has a plan. I'm fortunate enough to still be a part of this plan. I need to try hard (though tough at times) to remember all the things he gives me, rather than the few things that have been taken away from me temporarily right now. I haven't always appreciated the power of prayer, but truly believe that the prayers of many family and friends got me through what wasn't looking good for me, just a week ago. With continued prayer, I truly believe that we'll get back to having the things we need. Maybe we're also learning about some things that we don't need right now. I know everyone has their own thoughts on this topic, I'm living proof that I needed to be in the safest environment possible at my most vulnerable time, fighting for my life and then working on making my family stronger when I finally got home. I urge you to not waste this time. I ran out of time twice last week, only for God to put more time on the clock for me. I'm forever grateful of him, and I'm reminded constantly of a Matt Maher song "Lord, I Need

You." If you don't know it, do me a favor and listen to what has been my prayer. We all need him right now. God bless."

This sat on my phone for about an hour before I hit send. Part of me was thinking, *maybe it was just a good message for me to write, read, and delete.* The buzzing in my head of others telling me to share my story kept me from deleting it. I worried that some would take this as a political statement. I know that some people don't agree with the message or, at least, parts of it. I'm not saying I'm glad we are in quarantine, but more that with everything going on with the coronavirus, I am glad that people are restricted from just coming and going wherever they like. Obviously, I would've loved to see my wife and kids at the hospital, but it was worth me and them staying away from each other, and staying healthy, so I could get home quicker and spend that time with them.

After I hit send, I shut off my phone and watched the boys do something on the computer. I got what I needed off my chest. My story was slightly shared, and I urged people to make good use of their time if they were off.

Jen came back from wherever she was about a half hour later and said that she liked a response from the message I posted. I said I didn't see it and I hadn't looked at people's responses yet. Part of me wasn't looking for responses, but more to use my situation to help some people put this coronavirus into perspective. I told her I was nervous, as I feel I need to be doing something, I just don't know what it is. I don't know that I should be using my example in life as a message to other people. At what point does it become a "whoa-is-me" moment. When writing the message, I didn't even want to mention heart attack or fatal or time running out, but if you take that out of the post, it sounds like a typical person just ranting on a social media platform about the social distancing that many are frustrated with. I needed to throw that out there. Jen and I didn't advertise to people that I had a heart attack. Most people other than family found out by word of mouth as I can only imagine how hard it would've been for Jen to keep up if she would've sent a message to everyone in our lives.

As for the Matt Maher song "Lord, I Need You," this has been my go-to prayer most of the time during times that I've needed help, assurance, or comfort. This is by far my favorite Christian song and the words have always gotten me choked up a little bit. It doesn't matter what you are going through in life, this song is relevant to that. I sang it to myself a couple of times at the hospital and have listened to it multiple times since I've been home. I recommend everyone to put this in their music library.

*****

So, what needs to change in my life now? Before I figure out this plan or even if there is a special plan for me, I need to clean up some things. Even while at the hospital, the food menu had a little heart next to the items that I could eat. It started from day one. Coming home, I knew it wouldn't be any different. Jen had been trying for some time to get me more on whole grain or whole wheat items. I was now fair game to her thoughts and there was nothing I could do about it. We have been slowly working on different things that I will be able to eat. I am trying to wrap my head around that fact that most of this isn't temporary and that this is the first life change that needed to happen for me to sustain a healthier lifestyle.

The easy part right now is that I'm home for every meal. We have no practices, games, or tournaments right now, so we're home and can plan for all the meals. The first major challenge we will have with meals is when everything kicks back into full gear—I'm back to work, kids are back in school, and sports come back into our lives. The challenge of eating more than one meal a week together will be in full effect.

Like I mentioned, sports will eventually start up again soon. What are my priorities going to be with those? These take a ton of time out of my life which affects every person in our house. Something will need to give. I have some ideas of what should happen, and I will start steering my life towards those. Someone else or multiple people will have to step up and take some of the things off my plate. I am somewhat saddened on the fact of giving up some stuff that I was looking forward to doing for several years but am also excited about getting some of my time back to spend more on my own and with family and friends.

I also need to spend more time and focus on things with God. This plan is still lingering in the back of my head and it almost, at times, consumes me. Jen got a text from someone during this whole ordeal that said something like, "Maybe he pulled through this because you guys are so religious." I completely understand what this person was saying based on our friendship with them, but what does it mean to be religious? I believe in God. I believe he sent his son to save me from my sins. I believe that he will take care of me and eventually, return to take me home. We go to church every week, other than when there is a baseball tournament in summer, which the last couple of years has been every weekend. But what does religious mean?

I picture a religious person as an appointed leader of the church. Though Jen and I have taken on leadership roles at the church at different times, I don't feel I fall into that category. Being religious isn't because we believe. I think a lot of people believe and wouldn't ever be considered a religious person, maybe because of other actions, or because they don't regularly go to church. I don't personally believe that regularly going to church would make me or anyone a religious person. The church is not a building. A church is a where two or more gather to worship. That can be done at home, at the bar, in the barn, or at a baseball tournament. The church building itself is just that, a building. This is a common place for people to meet in larger groups and share their love and respect for God. I think, sometimes we get confused and think that going to the church building describes who we are with our relationship with Jesus Christ.

I would rather someone mention that maybe I have it well with the big guy upstairs because of faith. Faith is believing in something you've heard about but haven't seen for yourself. Faith is having a passion in something that you can't hold or touch. Faith is knowing that all I must do is believe in God and believe that Jesus came to save our sins. Faith is not about doing good works and trying to impress God. He wants us to do good things, be kind to others, support things that need support, but that isn't our path to heaven. Believing that Jesus died for my sins, rose from the dead, and will return is what will give me eternal salvation with him in heaven.

Good works are pleasing to God, so I must continue to do those. I must prioritize what I can do, what I can keep up with, and what I can do for the glory of him who created me. I was told a couple of times that God saved me because of the type of person I am. I don't find this to be true, as I believe I was saved this time because of the God he is. For all the things I've done wrong, said wrong, or thought wrong in my life, he had enough grace to save me before he is done with me.

Now, he's not done with me yet. So, I'm not done with him yet. Am I doing the right things in my Christian life to continue to please him? I will forever believe in him and what he has done for me, but I need to continue to do the appropriate things in my life to confirm to him that I love him, and I wanted to do well. It is my job to go and make disciples. I think some read that verse in the bible and think that Jesus was just talking to his disciples in that statement. He was talking to all of us. What can I do to bring people closer to God? That's been a hard thing for me to just bring up out of the blue in the past, but with a story now like mine, it might be easier for me to show my faith and hope that I can bring others to that same faith.

Again, this is all our jobs. It always has puzzled me when I'm at a church and the council or congregation are arguing about a pastor that isn't bringing in more people. How is this solely on a pastor? This is on all of us, equally. When is the last time you invited someone to church, a bible study, vacation bible school, Sunday school, a special holiday service, or maybe a potluck dinner at your church? I feel very disgusted every time someone puts this solely on the shoulders of a pastor and feel that we all have a hand in this game. Reach out. Show your faith. Be an example of what it is like to have Christ in your life. Invite.

*****

Three weeks later, I went back to work and have been working half days for a while. It's been good to get back to something normal. I continue to exercise more than needed and still eating healthy and avoiding the foods that I should not eat.

With the coronavirus, the kids will be at home for the remainder of the school season. Jen worked at home for a couple of months and then in June found out that her marketing job was being moved to Chicago. Though she was asked to move to Chicago to keep working, she turned that down, and her job ended in mid-July. After twenty years of working there, they gave her twenty weeks of pay, which allowed her to take her time to find the job and hours she wanted without feeling forced into something.

Jaicee eventually went back to working at the pizza market in town.

The boys' baseball seasons didn't look like they were going to happen at all, but after a late start and using precautions at practices, games, and tournaments, we were able to get in an abbreviated schedule and between the two of them still played in fifty-eight games. I still was a head baseball coach for two of the teams this season along with an assistant on the varsity team. Thankfully, everyone understood that my role needed to be reduced more than in the past. I let the other coaches run more of the practices and get more involved. I really did not help at all in any pregame scenarios, as they all just took that over. The head varsity coach also understood that I needed nights off at times, so was flexible on the nights that I was able to show up. So even though we got in a lot of games this year, my reduced role in all the teams was extremely refreshing and appreciated.

The first tournament I was back for to coach was for my bronco baseball boys that my oldest son plays on. This group of boys is extremely special to me, and it was extremely difficult to coach that day. We won our first two games and then lost to Medford in the championship. We did not have a ton of practices before we played in the tournament, but for the most part, the boys played well all day. After the games, as always, we met as a team to discuss the stuff we did good and then the stuff we need to work on. This was going to be just our normal type of speech, but at the last second, it changed to an extremely, difficult, emotional talk with my young friends. I ended up explaining to them that I just loved to watch them play because a couple of months before that, there was a chance that I was never going to see them play again, let alone coach them. I knew some of the boys were aware of what happened, but not all of them knew much.

We really did not discuss much about the actual tournament that day. Outside of a few things that we discussed about what we will work on moving forward, it really was more about their effort that needs to be put in every time they put on their cleats, step on a field, and put their equipment in the dugout. Enjoy the moments you get to play. Enjoy the moments with your friends. Use every opportunity as a learning moment. Lastly, leave everything out on the field or court or mat or wherever on whatever you are doing. All I wanted from them is an effort in what they were doing. All I wanted from them was them showing me that effort so I can even enjoy their games more than ever. I also wanted them to know how important it was for me to be there and still be their coach. It was a hard talk to go through, but as they head off to high school now, they are at the age that some of this needs to start sinking in. I do not believe in equal playing time at certain levels or situations. Equal playing time typically only rewards those that do not put in the time outside of games on their own. Moving forward, their work ethic and how they prepare when a coach is not around and when there is not a practice will determine who will play or not. I want them all on the field when it is time to play, but they need to realize that is on them now and not on a coach.

I did decide to give up a basketball opportunity that I was looking forward to doing. With the plans of still coaching the sixth-grade boys team this year, I decided that I did not want to do double duty yet this year to see how things went. Hopefully, an opportunity will come up again in the future.

After several weeks of working about four hours a day, I slowly got that to six hours per day and finally up to seven to eight hours a day. Though those would not be considered full days from what I was used to, I am still extremely exhausted after that length of day right now.

I have had just one doctor appointment since I have been back to work. When the doctor walked into the room that day, he looked at me and said, "I didn't tell you that you had to lose all that weight." I told him that "the diet you put me on kind of told me to lose some weight." Without sugars and salt in my diet, I have been able to lose about fifty-five pounds as of my six-month anniversary of my heart attack which I just celebrated in September.

I have continued to eat healthy and consistent with what the plan is. I am still on four medications, and the eating plan and medicine plan are in full effect until at least March of 2021, which is when my next appointment will be.

People are constantly asking how I feel and applaud me on my weight loss. Though I thought those questions moving forward were going to bother me, I enjoy being asked. Not to talk about myself, but it gives me a chance to tell people that care about me a little bit about my story.

As I mentioned before, it also gives me a small opportunity to share my strengthened faith through this whole process and share with them that God is good. If this is my new responsibility and my situation gives me an easier opportunity to maybe get God in someone else's life, than that is what I'm trying to do. If this isn't what the plan was going to be, then I guess I'm just doing it on my own, and maybe if I can just continue to share my feel-good story with others, they can come to their own conclusions about the greatness of God, with maybe a little help from me sharing what I went through.

For now, I am good. My body is tired much of the time. Not like the "I didn't get enough sleep" tired, just feel wore down constantly. Every once in a while, I can still feel what seems to be the rib pain yet, and lately, I've had muscle soreness that comes and goes, which I've heard from multiple people now, is common with the medications that I'm still taking.

I will take all of that over the alternative that was almost a reality. I can do things and spend times with my family. I am still coaching sports and playing basketball with my boys. I have a better appreciation for the people in my life and the things I need in my life. I have a better understanding of the things I can do without in my life and not be disappointed with those. Every time I get to see my friends and coach a sport, it gives me a higher appreciation to the relationships that come with that. Life is good and will only get better from here.

*****

That's my story. I scared a lot of people when I didn't even know what was going on myself. The power of prayer that I've questioned for a very long time, seems to have got me through this time and has made me believe how powerful it is. I cannot believe the love and support that Jen, my kids, and I have had during this time.

This story doesn't end though. The easy things are making sure I reach out to the people that stepped up and thank them. In the past, this is probably the end of the story. This time, it isn't. I need to continue to eat healthy to make sure I recover completely and sustain that for the years to come, so I can stay healthy and out of a high-risk situation. Though my previous health only played a small part in this hereditary situation, it will still help keep the risk of this happening again down.

I need to prioritize some of the extracurricular things in my life and step away from some of them. This will give me the appropriate time to wind down more and rest. This will allow me to help others get involved and feel the same satisfaction I've felt from getting involved and volunteering my time to my community.

I need to continue working and practicing how to pray. There is no right way or wrong way, as long as you are just having a conversation with God. This may include talking to him. This may be just asking him some questions. I may still recite the lyrics of Christian songs, including "Lord, I Need You." I need to understand that he will answer the prayers. It may not be right away. It may not be the answer I want. It may not be clear on what his response is. Sometimes the relationship you have with God allows you to discuss things with someone when it is extremely difficult to discuss with others.

I want to get back to having relationships with friends and family that have been missing from my life for many years. Sometimes things are said or done in relationships that weren't meant, taken out of context, said by gossip, and simply aren't true, yet they've torn apart relationships while one side doesn't even know why. Getting back in touch with old friends, some that maybe need to hear my story, and becoming a person that talks more about the grace of God and how I got through this. We need God so much right now, with everything that is going on in this world, and maybe some people just need a little kickstart to start moving their lives that direction.

I need to consider where I need to be with my kids more and be more a part of their personal individual life. Going to their sporting events or coaching them in sports is not really spending quality time with them. Everything I'm doing with one of them, I'm completely shutting out the other two. My daughter will soon be going away to college. What actual time have I spent with her that was meaningful to both of us? We try to go out a couple of times a year, just the two of us, but what is that really: small chitchat while we're eating out somewhere. We took a great trip to Lifest Christian Music Festival last year and hope to do that again in the future.

And then there is Jen. It, again, is extremely important to have a good working and communicating relationship with your spouse. That relationship typically makes a lot of the other things tick. Our relationship hasn't always worked the best and we haven't always communicated well, and it won't always happen moving forward. One thing that we need to commit to each other though is that we keep trying. Keep doing this together.

By staying together and working harder on this will also pull us closer together to a passion that both of us have in our lives—God. We don't love him or thank him near enough. He has helped us out of things we don't even know we were in. He answers prayers that we haven't prayed yet and maybe, weren't planning on praying for. Regardless of the struggles of the world right now. Regardless of me having a heart attack. Regardless of our kids growing so fast before our eyes and will be soon be off doing what they want to do with life. Regardless if we question God's responses to prayers. Regardless if we are with friends or quarantined from them. I know that "Lord, I Need You":

Lord, I come, I confess. / Bowing here, I find my rest. / Without you, I fall apart. / You're the One, that guides my heart. / Lord I need you, oh I need you. / Every hour I need you. / My one defense, my righteousness. / Oh God, how I need you. / Where sin runs deep, your grace is more. / Where grace is found, is where you are. / Where you are, Lord I am free. / Holiness is Christ in me. / Lord I need you, oh I need you. / Every hour I need you. / My one defense, my righteousness. / Oh God, how I need you. / So teach my song, to rise to you. / When temptation comes my way. / When I cannot stand, I'll fall on you. / Jesus, you're my hope and stay. / Lord I need you, oh I need you. / Every hour I need you. / My one defense, my righteous- ness. / Oh God, how I need you. / You're my one defense, my righteousness. / Oh God, how I need you. / My one defense, my righteousness. / Oh God, how I need you. (Matt Maher,2013; from "All the People Said Amen")

God bless you everyone. On to the next chapter of life and moving forward with a much higher appreciation for the power of prayer. A lot of good things can come after a painful situation, and I am living proof of that.

End

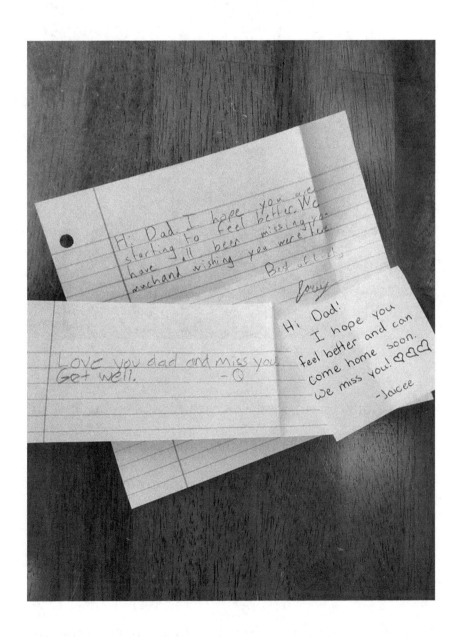

About the Author

Ron Kunkel is a happily married man of eighteen years. A father of three amazing kids. A follower and believer in Jesus Christ. A devoted person to the community and the kids within it. While coaching multiple youth teams, he spends much of the year juggling family, work, church and sports, but he wouldn't change it for the world. Things happen for a reason, so when they do it isn't about the why it happened, it's about the "what's next?"